Uncommon Service

When doing the Uncommon thing leads to success!

Dedication

To my incredible husband and children who have stood beside me during all the years on my journey. Thank you for believing in me and my dreams.

Disclaimer

Limit of Liability/Disclaimer of Warranty: While the author has used her best efforts in preparing this book, she makes no representations or warranties with respect to accuracy or completeness of the contents of this book and specifically disclaims any implied warranties of merchantability or fitness for a particular purpose. No warranty may be created or extended by sales representatives or written sales materials. The advice and strategies contained herein may not be suitable to your situation. You should consult with a professional where appropriate. The author shall not be liable for any loss of profit or any other commercial damages, including but not limited to special, incidental, consequential, or other damages.

All rights reserved. No part of this book may be reproduced or transmitted in any form or by any means, electronic or mechanical, including photocopying, recording or by information storage and retrieval system without written permission from the author, except for the inclusion of brief quotation in review.

Copyright 2024 by Cheryl Law

Prologue

What is uncommon service? Uncommon service is old-fashioned service. It's the service we used to get when we went to a family general store.

Growing up in a small town I remember Saturday mornings at the local stores. My Mom and I would walk into the grocery store and the owner would come over, shake my mom's hand and give me a giant smile followed by a penny candy. If something wasn't on the shelf that we needed, they would gladly go check the stock room to be sure that it hadn't come in on today's shipment. As we went through the till the cashier would always ask about family or chat about good things happening in town.

I remember one particular Saturday being curious because the grocery's belt would go all the way around behind the clerk, so she took me and showed me her pedal and even let me try it.

When was the last time a business made you feel like that?

That feeling is uncommon service!

I can already hear you saying that is unrealistic. The owner of the store rarely is at the store nowadays and the computer system controls all the stock. You are correct but does it have to be the owner to make a customer feel like that? I don't think it does.

Through this book, I'm going to tell you stories of uncommon and today's common service. We will break down what the difference is and how you can implement it in your business or your service.

Table of Contents

Section One 6
    Scenario One 7
    Scenario Two 15
    Scenario Three 22
    Scenario Four 25
    Scenario Five 29
    Scenario Six 33
    Scenario Seven 36
    Scenario Eight 40
    Scenario Nine 44
    Scenario Ten 48
    Scenario Eleven 52
    Scenario Twelve 55
    Scenario Thirteen 57
    Scenario Fourteen 59
    Scenario Fifteen 61

Section Two 64
    Conclusion 73
    Bonus 76

Section One

Scenario One

This book had been rolling around in my head for a while, but it recently became clearer to me that old-fashioned customer service has become uncommon. I also clearly saw that uncommon service is needed in today's digital marketplace to prevent our customers from purchasing elsewhere.

Growing up in a small town, I was very aware that by purchasing locally or as local as we could and supporting the smaller stores, we were buying from our neighbours and their families, putting food on their tables and clothes on their backs.

Every fall we change out the filter for the hot tub and one would think that it would be easy to buy a filter. In the last few years, we have been finding it a challenge.

As a consumer who likes to purchase locally, I made a trip to our closest hot tub store. We had bought our hot tub from here, but it happens to be about 35 min from my home. I had a couple of other errands to run so I didn't call first.

When I walked in there were two ladies in the store at the counter. I walked up to the counter, and she said hello with a smile that never really got to her eyes. I said, "I need a filter for our hot tub" and looked over my shoulder at the filters. I said "I don't see it there. It is the big one. Are you out of stock?"

This is a single brand store, so it only carries about 6 different filters.

She looked at me and said, "Everything we have is on the shelf." in a rather snarky tone. Then added "Everyone changes their filters in the fall."

The other lady who had been off to the side organizing came over and said "I think we may have one of those in the back but it's for someone else. I don't know when he is coming to get it though."

The clerk at the counter then said, "I have more coming In. They might be here tomorrow."

Frustrated by this point I let her know I was 35 minutes away and didn't want to make a special trip the next day. She didn't say anything, so I asked her if she could put my name on it and call me when it was in order to prevent making another wasted trip and I could tell this was an inconvenience. She asked if we were in the system, found our names and said, "I'll call you."

I still wanted to change the water out in my hot tub that weekend and got thinking as I was driving home that there was another little Hot tub store in a neighbouring town and decided to call there.

On the phone the young man was polite and eager to help. He said "We don't deal with that brand but if I had a part number or the filter I can check and see if we have that filter on the shelf."

I told him "I was about 10 min away and would most likely recognize it so I would stop in."

I confirmed with him that they were still in the same building, and he said no and gave me directions to the new location.

When I arrived, I realized they were very busy that day. They also filled water and there was a store full of people. I stood back and waited my turn. When it was my turn, I explained who I was, and we went over to the shelf. I didn't see the filter there so he asked me if I could wait a minute because his boss might know, and they had more in the back. I described the filter and they said "Do you know the model of the tub? " which I didn't, so I quickly called my husband and got the model. It didn't come up in their listings so we both started to google the model and found it on Amazon.

The young man said, "You can order from there or I did find it in my system, and it would arrive on Tuesday." I told him I like to shop locally and as long as the price was going to be the same, I would wait for it to come in. He said that they had a lady who placed their orders the next day and he took my name and phone number with the part number and thanked me for wanting to support a small business like his. Happy with the answers I let my husband know what I had found. Since we weren't going to be able to do it that night.

On Tuesday I waited all day, but no call came. Thinking that maybe the shipment was late I waited until the end of the day Wednesday and then called. The lady asked my name and said that she had seen the note, and she was the one who placed the orders - but that she hadn't ordered it because she didn't see the part number and didn't have my number to confirm the order. If I brought in the filter, she could get the number off the filter.

I told her "No, that I had already figured out that information with the last person and that I would just order it off Amazon."

I then ordered the filter from Amazon which said it would be another two weeks and unlike most addresses can't come directly to my door. My thoughts were that if the original store called in the meantime, I would save myself this headache in the spring by having an extra filter.

Another week later the forecast was calling for snow before the filter would show up, so I called the original store to see if any had come in. When I asked, she said "Yes, we have them on the shelf." They hadn't saved one under our name and never called to tell us they were in.

This is the service I feel like I get more often than not. I also hear staff and business owners around me talk about competing with Amazon and how the customers keep buying online vs in the stores. Why do you think they have started to purchase more online? It's simple - it takes time and money to come to a store in person and if the service is subpar what makes them want to spend their time and money?

Let's take a look at how the story above could have been one of Uncommon Service, instead of a complete disappointment.

- Basic service would have been to have the hot tub filter on the shelf to start with. In this case, I know the lady behind the counter happened to be the store owner. She told me that this time of year these filters sell faster. Would it not make sense to bring in extra filters during high seasons for changing the hot tub water?

Ok, so there was a big run on filters. What else could they have done to try to satisfy my needs?

- If they had one left and didn't know when the other customer was coming in to get it, could they have called the other person and asked when he was coming in? If he said it wasn't for a day or two, could they have then asked him if it would be okay if they sold it to someone from out of town and reordered to have it there before he came in? I find if you ask questions in most cases people are reasonable as long as you communicate with them.

- The hot tub store could have offered to ship the filter to me (for a small fee) when it came in, to save me a trip. If I order something from Amazon even if it says free shipping, it's likely included in the price.

- Call me when it does come in. This is basic service and or call me when there is an issue with what you were asked to order instead of making me wait, then call and find out on my own. It doesn't even have to be a call; it can be a text.

UNCOMMON SERVICE

What could the hot tub company do to create the uncommon service like store owners of the past?

The store owners of the past used to know their customers and most times had a good idea of their needs and wants.

Every person who buys a hot tub from the store is entered on the computer. The store knows what hot tub they bought and if they keep track of purchases, they know what filter and when you bought it from them. If you know that you see an influx of filter sales in the fall and spring, you could reach out to the customers by phone to better plan your inventory.

"Hi George, It's. Cheryl from ABC Hot Tub. I was just planning for my fall filter order. Will you be needing a filter for your hot tub this fall? I want to make sure I have adequate stock for my customers and by preplanning we get extra discounts from the manufacturer that help us keep our pricing low for you."

I can already hear you saying, "Cheryl you're crazy, I don't have time to do this!"

What most people don't realize is this kind of uncommon service could create unquantifiable sales you didn't know were out there.

Here are some of the responses you will get.

- "I do need that filter that would be great"
  - » Your response could be "Perfect I will have it here for you. Do you need anything else at the same time?"
- "I will need the filter and I'm getting low on my chemicals as well"
  - » Your response "Sounds great, what chemicals were you looking for? I'm placing an order for them as well."
- "I don't own that hot tub anymore, I sold it."
  - » "I'm sorry to hear that. Did you replace it, or do you know the people you sold it to?"
- "Actually, it quit working, but I was going to try to find someone to fix it"
  - » "We have a great service technician. Would you like me to put it into his schedule?"
- "I was thinking about trading it for a new one, I heard these saltwater systems are better."
  - » "We can certainly help you with that. Do you have time to chat now or would you like me to send you some information?"
- "Sorry I don't live near you anymore. We moved the tub when we moved."
  - » "OK, no worries, do you still have the tub? We do offer shipping to your door?"

What advantages do these responses give you?

- You can better plan your inventory if only 5 of those tubs are left in your area you don't need 30 filters.
- You also have an idea of what chemicals are usually sold when they buy filters.
- It can very quickly give you a boost in service work.

Customers take the path of least resistance. When we make it easy to do business with them, they become more likely to do business with us.

And the best part is how many people will tell their friends. "You know what, I got a call today from my hot tub store. They wanted to make sure they have what I need for fall, I hate waiting for stuff to come. They even offered to ship them when they came in."

Most people will attempt to do something like this; they will send out an email saying order now to their customers. Will that email give you the information to update your files? Will it create the same caring feeling, or will it feel like they are being sold to vs being cared about?

Scenario Two

The difference between uncommon customer service and poor customer service is the feelings it evokes within the customer.

I challenge you to think about your memories. What do you remember from the favourite places you visit?

Going back to that small town I grew up in, we had a little gas station. I remember going in there and the dust and dirt were an inch thick, but the owner of that store was one of the nicest guys you would ever meet. I was responsible for mowing the lawn at home with our ride-on lawn mower and I had a little motorbike that I spent hours riding around the yard or over to the neighbours to ride with with a friend. I could pull up to the pumps at the gas station with my motorbike and sometimes I would have my wagon hitched on behind it with a Jerry can to fill the lawn mower with. The owner would wipe his hand on the rag he kept in his overalls and come fill it up, he then would put it on my dad's charge account and off I would go with a wave and a smile. Some days he would even give me a couple of quarters to get a pop out of the old machine inside.

I'm not saying put your business at risk by offering credit. That's what we have debit and credit cards for now. What I am saying is now the store owners don't pump your gas and if I showed up on my motorbike pulling a wagon with a Jerry can they probably wouldn't fill it. I do know that he gave me the best service he could. I go back to the fact that the store wasn't very clean. That doesn't matter -what mattered was that he made everyone feel at home. I even remember him fixing tires for the people in town and if you had a flat on the weekend, he would be the first one to open his doors to get you going again.

One Friday we were headed to a Rodeo for the weekend, and I was supposed to ride that night. As it always seemed to happen, we had a flat tire on the trailer. Dad rushed to get it jacked up and when he pulled the spare out it was flat too, we quickly loaded them up and headed to the local gas station. The owner was just locking the door. In today's common service most likely you would be told "Sorry we are Closed I will fix it tomorrow." Instead, the words we got were, "You're just in time if it would have been a few minutes later you would have had to call me.". He was telling us that even if he had gone home for the day, he would have come back to fix them. And his after-hours number was on the door.

We got fixed up and Dad got the tire back on the trailer, while I stowed the spare in the compartment, and we were on the way.

Have you ever had a store owner yell across the store that was closing in 5 min or had that staff member taping the till at 10 min before closing? I get that we all have long days and want to get home to our family or friends, but it is our job to service our customers and without them, we don't have a business.

I was recently in a store right as they were getting ready to close. It had been a long day, and I was way behind schedule, but this was the only time I had to get what I needed before the weekend. It is a store where I frequently buy paint for fixing furniture. The lady who took care of the paints stayed an extra 30 min to show me some products because I was having a hard time deciding what I needed. She was patient and helpful and because of that, they are my go-to store anytime I need any paint products. There are some cheaper bargain stores, but I will pay for the service I get at this particular store because they offer me uncommon service.

My daughter got an email on Christmas Eve that a present she had been waiting for to give her sister had arrived at the pick-up location she called to find out they closed at 7 pm. Rushing out the door to go the 40 min to the location it had been shipped to she arrived at 6:50. When she got to the counter she told the lady what she was there for and the lady looked at her and didn't take her name and said "ok" and headed into the back. 10 min later she came back out and by this time it's 7, closing time and there is a line of 5 people. She was empty handed and flipped her closed sign on the pick-up counter.

My daughter said, "Excuse me, did you get my package?" The lady ignored her.

Then another lady in the line asked if she was going to help them and they got told by the clerk, "No, if you had planned better, you wouldn't be in this predicament."

My daughter said, "I got the notice at 6 and drove 40 min to get here and I called to see what time you closed."

The rest of the people also said similar things like they only got the notice at 6 and came as quickly as they could.

"Well, that's too bad." the clerk said as she walked away. One lady was in tears. It was her daughter's only Christmas gift that she had been waiting weeks for.

How hard would it have been to get the items? If she had gotten my daughter's item, she would have had it before the store even closed but the clerk chose not to help her. And now another young girl may never believe in Santa because someone had a bad day or didn't feel like being helpful. I don't even know the other 3 stories, but they are similar, I'm sure.

I know we get those customers who always call right at the end of the day or come in just as we close. Here's another way to think about it.
- They could choose a store that stays open later
- Or one closer to where they are going.
- Maybe they had already gotten home and realized they needed one more thing
- Maybe they couldn't get someone to watch the kids earlier
- They could have gotten off work late too.

For example, my daughter had a gig coming up. She is a musician and decided at the last minute she needed a new pair of pants for her gig. the next day. Yes, bad planning on our part, so she called me and told me that she wanted to run in and get some jeans from the local western store at the end of work. I was sitting in the parking lot waiting for her at the place we agreed to meet when I got a text stating that her truck wouldn't start. Her boss had helped her get it started, but she was running way behind, and we were nervous to park it where we were going to meet for fear of it not starting again. She has a local garage that's been doing the repairs on our vehicles, so we decided to park the vehicle there. While I was waiting for her to arrive at the garage, I called the store to see if they even had the type of pants she was looking for. This local western store happens to have two locations in town and the location I called did not have stock, but instead of just sending me to the other location she said. "Just one minute I'm going to put you on hold and I'm going to call the other store for you." She called the other store and came back on the phone to let me know that they didn't have exactly what we were looking for, but they had two or three other options at that store. I confirmed that they closed in an hour and thanked her for her time. Knowing that things were going to be a little tight, I talked to my daughter and we made a game plan about how we were going to make this all work in our timelines. We dropped her vehicle off at the local shop and called the store back. I let them know that I would be coming in right at 5 which was when they closed and would it be OK if we still came. The lady on the phone hesitated for a moment but then said "Yes, no problem we'll keep our doors open please try to be here as quickly as possible."

When we arrived at the store there were still a couple of other customers in the store so we didn't feel quite as rushed as we thought we would. My daughter found what she was looking for very quickly and then the store owner said, "You know I have new arrivals in the back you may like these better." and went to get them. When he came back, he handed her another pair. She ended up with the set that the store owner gave her because they fit so much better than the other ones.

And not only were they friendly and courteous but they also asked if we'd gotten the vehicle taken care of. Had we not gotten into the store that night my daughter wouldn't have had new stage clothes. Would it have been the end of the world? Maybe not, but it is worth the confidence the clothes give her.

We don't know most of our customer's stories and usually don't strike up enough of a conversation to find out.

I like to make it my goal to get to know my customers. The more you listen and learn from your customers, the better you can serve them.

If they had been mad or unwilling to help because we were at the store right at closing time, they wouldn't have ended up with a sale at all because the pants she thought she wanted for her performance did not look the way they did on the model and would have made her feel self-conscious during the performance. However, the jeans the store owner gave her made her feel strong and beautiful. We didn't even look at the price, but they were a high-end brand that cost around $200. Is $200 worth an extra 10 min to stay open? I certainly believe it is. And what would the cost have been if we had gone to another store that gave us better service? As a family we spend close to $5000 a year on clothes from this particular store, would we start shopping elsewhere? Maybe.

An example of uncommon service:
They were prepared to stay a few minutes late to keep a customer happy.

They took the time to offer other suggestions even though it was near the end of the day.

One of the things this store does well is finding your needs and figuring out the best way to fulfill them. For example: I bought jeans for my husband and the jeans were at one store but not the other. They would even have a staff member run them between stores while you're there. Guess what happens? I'm always really happy and I usually end up looking around long enough that I buy extra. Proving once again that Uncommon service will increase your profits as well as loyalty.

Scenario Three

I go back to the part of the story where my daughter's truck wouldn't start. We come from a mechanically inclined family and my husband could have fixed the issues with the truck. We were pretty sure the starter had a dead spot in it because you had lots of power to the starter and if you banged the starter it would move through and start later. The starter was easier to change on the hoist, so that night when we dropped it off at the local shop, I let the shop owner know that we just needed the starter replaced. Also, I told him if he was going to be able to get to it in the next couple of days, we were going to leave it but if not, we would take it home until he could get it in.

He said to me "Let me look at my schedule - give me one second." and went back to check. When he came back, he said "Leave it with me, I will get it fixed up and I will call her when it's ready."

He made it simple - he didn't make us jump through any hoops; he just took care of it. The next morning, I got a call from the reception desk of the shop saying that it was ready. We had dropped it off at 5:00 the night before. This was 8:00 AM. When the store closes at 5 and opens at 8, how did they get it done that fast? The receptionist told me that they had been booking two weeks out and that the only way to get us taken care of was for the technician to come in early, which he gladly did and got her fixed up and on the road. I let them know they hadn't needed to do that, but it was greatly appreciated. Their quick prompt service is the reason we promote them as one of the go-to shops. The more we promote them the harder it is for us to get taken care of, but we want our friends and family around us to have that same kind of service. That day when we picked up our vehicle, to show them our appreciation, we brought them breakfast sandwiches from the local store.

The uncommon service in this is that most people aren't willing to go that extra mile. If you want to give your customers uncommon service all you need to do is look outside the box and see what types of things can be done to help them out.

Scenario Four

I was in a large box store today picking up a couple of last-minute things for Halloween. As I'm coming through the self-checkouts (I won't get into that yet), the person responsible was off at a distance watching. She wasn't watching me to ensure I scanned everything, she was watching because the box store had added another question to the list of checkout questions. The question was, did everything scan properly for you today and did you scan any bags? Me being me, I just hit "no" all the time to the barrage of questions I get asked at the tills. The question sent me back to the previous screen. She could see my frustration and by the time she came over, the till had asked the question again and already reset so I was able to put my card in. Instead of being annoyed, she said to me, "Yup, they added a new question to slow us all down," and laughed.

She was trying to have fun with something that she could have easily let take her day in a completely wrong direction.

I was thinking about the question the box store was asking and it annoys me that they ask me to scan my own items and then ask me if I scanned everything. If you don't trust me to scan everything then why am I scanning my own stuff?

I guess it is time to talk about self-checkouts. As a businessperson, I understand the purpose behind them. I do feel it loses the personal touch a store can have and if I'm going through the self-checkout and staff asks me if I need help why didn't I just have a till to go through? Yes, I rarely have to stand in line to wait, but by the time I find all the barcodes and remember if it's a vegetable or fruit to look it up, then weigh my items I could have had someone else scan it all.

Today the store had one regular till open and 6 self-checkouts. There were 3 staff standing watching the self-checkouts. That means only one person would have had to stand in line at each till. I would gladly do that to see a smile and get asked how my day was or how old my child is. That's no extra cost for the same service.

Our local grocery store still has cashiers, and they are always cheerful and friendly. The staff are hired for the position by their demeanour and not just put there even if they aren't good with people. Both of my daughters worked at this store. They hired a lot of students, and it was their first job. I was always impressed with their training program. They were taught what was expected of them, not just given an employee package and said, "Here go do your job." There were some rules in place that seemed to be rigid, but these rules were also to ensure the customers got the best service they could.

I asked others for their stories on recent customer experiences. This one stood out as an opportunity to give uncommon service versus the service they received. I know we all have stories like this one.

I was in a grocery store in the cracker section. We stood there for several minutes obviously trying to find what we were looking for (toasted baguettes). The whole time there was an employee beside us stocking boxes of crackers and didn't offer any help. I finally asked about the baguettes, and he said he didn't know because he doesn't work in that department. My jaw dropped I think as I looked at the boxes of crackers in his hand. Well, it sure liked like he did.

In the local store I was talking about above, they would never have allowed this to happen. If the staff member was unsure, they had instructions to find someone that did know. Maybe the person in question was new and was thinking baguettes are a bakery item, I can't say for sure, but my friend would have been less disappointed if the staff member had said. "I'm not positive but let me ask someone, or I'm new but let me go find out, or I'm sorry, I'm not employed by the store, but the cracker company."

I remember looking for a special pretzel crisp my daughter's friends had recently had. We went up and down the aisle 3 times looking for them and couldn't find them, we asked one of the staff and their response was perfect. "Oh, I love those, they should be in the cracker aisle."

I mentioned to her that we had looked there and couldn't find them. "Let's go look," she said as she walked over to the spot where she thought they were and there was none there. "Hmm, that's weird. I know we carry them. Let me go check the stock room." When she came back said, "They moved them into the gluten-free aisle," and instead of walking away she came over to the aisle with us to make sure we found them. This was a little thing and may have felt insignificant to the staff member, but it made us feel like we mattered enough to see it through.

When you compare these two examples. What is the difference between common service and uncommon service?

Care and attention: If this store had just said "Not my job," "I don't know," or "Down the cracker aisle." We would have never found the item and it would have cost the store not only the sale that day, but we still put this item in our cart almost every other trip to the store.

When was the last time a stock person asked if you needed help while they were putting away stock? Or helps us short people get something from the top shelf?

Scenario Five

In the dealership I worked at there was a policy that if you were within 5 feet of someone you smiled, said hello, good morning, or engaged them in a conversation. This simple act made our customers feel welcome in the store.

I remember my mom talking about hating my favourite store. Why did our opinions vary so much?

When I went into the store, I found the staff was always friendly, warm, welcoming, and helpful but my mom had one bad experience and it turned her off. She felt like the staff was following her around the store because of the way the store was laid out, they couldn't see their customers and the staff member was following her but not engaging her in conversation it made her feel like they thought that she was a shoplifter.

Customers need to feel welcome in a store or business. When they don't, they either opt to purchase online or somewhere that makes them feel wanted and needed.

Look at your business and decide what things you can do to make the customer feel appreciated. Most don't even have to cost you money.

- Smile and say hello
- Ask if they need help finding something
- Thank them for shopping with you

- If they don't buy anything say, "See you again."
- If something is coming on sale the following week let them know before they purchase or better yet give them the discount early
- Thank you cards or emails are a great way to show appreciation. You can even include a discount for their next visit

Many stores offer a service instead of a product. In the past, these were the businesses that offered better service than others. Today you will find that getting even basic service has become a challenge because just doing enough has become the norm, but these are also the businesses that need to give better service.

The generation that is being raised right now hasn't experienced customer service in the same way we have. Everything they do has been technology-based. While technology can be a great thing, it has also made the world more impersonal.

Just today I got a call from the Spa that does my massages. She was calling to confirm that I was going to make my appointment the next day. I also got a text from them about an hour later. While I was thinking to myself It seemed crazy to do both, I looked back at my theory of uncommon service and realized what this spa was doing was uncommon. Calling me was a courtesy and it also protected their business because they were able to reduce the number of no-shows they had. The text was a backup in place by the owner in case they didn't have the time to make the calls that day or the staff chose not to complete their jobs. The business still had checks and balances.

This isn't the only company that does this. My dog groomer gives me the same call as does my Physio.

Life gets so busy, and we forget appointments.

If you have 3 staff working and they take a customer every 30 min. That is 48 phone calls to make this appears to be a lot but if you narrow it down it isn't. If it takes 1. Min average per customer to call and confirm the appointment that's less than 1 hour out of the day to make these calls. Can you honestly say that the receptionist can't find 10 min per hour to make this courtesy call for an appointment?

Scenario Six

I have a customer that no one else wants to deal with. They said, "He was unreasonable and rude."

The first time I sat down with the customer I made sure I truly listened to him and asked him questions regarding his concerns.

When he started he just said "I hate dealing with your company", so I asked him why, and he told me about an issue he was having that wasn't resolved. Then we went through the issue and discussed a solution. He agreed to the solution and went on to ask, "Then what can you do about this problem?" Because I had given him a solution to one of his small issues, he opened up about another concern. By the time we finished the conversation he had let me know about 6 issues that all seemed rather small. But as you compiled them made the customer feel like we didn't care about him.

I took the time to listen then build a plan and solution. To this day I still laugh because I was told the customer doesn't spend money he just complains. Now that I have a clear idea of his expectations and I have checks and balances in place to resolve them, this customer has tripled his expenditure with the company. Was taking the time to resolve the issue worth it? To me it was and I always like to be able to say "I turned that relationship around, he is good to deal with."

One question I get a lot is. "How can you give great service when you work remotely?" I completed all of the above while working remotely. My best piece of advice is keep doing all the things in this book. You don't need to be in person to give great service, you just need to care. Communication becomes even more important when you work remotely.

Have you ever noticed that when we have difficult customers someone new comes along to help them and is able to resolve the issue. Many times, it is because the person who is new to the conversation is looking at it from a different angle than the people who have already been involved. Can you remove your feelings from the situation and look at it from another angle, the same way a person who is new to the situation would?

Scenario Seven

The waitress that writes things down, the customer service agent that takes notes while they are talking to you. An order taker. Many of us have great memories while some of us forget it the minute we walk away.

Some people feel it takes too much work to write it down, but you will have way fewer mistakes if you do.

A large group of us went for supper the other night. When we first arrived, we were seated right away. She gave us great seats to be close to the live music. The waitress had multiple tables and ours was a table that likes to have a few drinks with our meals.

She took all our original orders and those came out quickly and with accuracy. One of the gentlemen at the table was a craft beer drinker so he asked what beers they had on tap. Instead of telling him or giving him a list, she said, "The list is above the bar." This was not visible from where we were sitting.

We placed our meal orders, and she wrote them down. The waitress then went to enter our orders and didn't come back again until the food came out. By then our drinks were empty and as the food came out someone else was bringing it. As there was nothing written for where each of the meals went, they just started asking who had what, and meals got placed in front of the wrong people because some of us ordered the same thing in different variations. Once they got that all straightened out, we asked for more drinks. The waitress said no problem and took the orders - unfortunately only delivering half of them. We asked again for those drinks, as the night progressed, and we ordered more drinks sometimes we would get them sometimes we might not. When our friend asked for a sample of one of the craft beers after he'd gone up to the bar and looked at the chart, she got really upset. As the night went on the service continued to get worse and worse. We had designated drivers - one of whom was me, so I requested a coffee. She kindly said "I'm going to make a new pot. I'll be out with it in a few minutes. " I asked for that same coffee three times but never received it. Our table seemed to quit getting served. Unlikely we will return there.

The following week my daughter and I went to another restaurant. As we sat down the waitress was at the table immediately with a menu. The place was packed, and we got the last table because on Wednesdays they do wing night. She quickly took our drink orders and told us she would be a few minutes before she got back to take our food orders. We chatted for a little while and the waitress quickly came back and took our food orders. It wasn't very long before she came back to take the next drink order. I was meeting some friends, and they were starting to arrive. My daughter decided she was going to go just as our food came out of the kitchen. She asked if the food could be packaged up in a takeout container and the waitress did not hesitate at all. She quickly went into the back and packaged the food up for her and she was on her way. We ended up switching tables and there were no complaints from the waitress at all about this. She just happily took care of us. There was nothing extraordinary about her service - it was just good service. She appreciated us being there. My friends and I frequently go to this restaurant and the service we receive is typically like this. The waitresses even take the time to ask about family and friends.

I know this is a smaller restaurant. But even if you're a server in a larger restaurant there are many opportunities for you to build rapport and give above and beyond service. As a waitress, have you ever asked your table if they're celebrating something or what brings them out tonight. Maybe it's a new job. Maybe it's a birthday. Maybe it's just a date night. Most times when somebody goes to a restaurant it's something important to them. Then find a way to tie that to the conversation or congratulate them on their anniversary. Small gestures go a long way. Some restaurants do free cakes or desserts on birthdays. Maybe it's a glass of wine for an anniversary.

If it's not a special day, find something to say like "Oh I love your coat", or "What a lovely family you have." Compliments are a simple way to build rapport. They need to be natural - they can't come in a fake manner. For example, if you say "Nice coat", it sounds kind of fake. If you say "I love the colour or the style of your coat" it gives them a reason to understand why you're complimenting them, making it feel more natural and more special.

One of the things I hear all the time is I don't have time to do the things that are recommended. I barely have time to do the job I need to do. When you compliment someone how long does it take 5 minutes 10 minutes? I don't think it takes more than a few seconds. That 10 seconds can make a difference in someone's day.

Scenario Eight

When you're having a bad day do you take it out on others around you? What type of things does it take to make you feel better?

For me some of those things are as simple as a smile. Maybe I just got in a fight with my spouse and needed to get out of the house and I was projecting some of my anger back on you. I believe that you catch more flies with honey than vinegar.

Does this give you the right to be abused at work no, but I do believe how we react to the situation can make a positive impact on that person's day. When you have a grumpy customer, step back from the situation and decide "Did I create this situation?" If the answer is 'yes' you need to quickly look for a resolution. If the answer is 'no" you need to find a way to kill them with kindness.

There are many techniques for mirroring that help pull the customer out of a situation like this for example, if their arms are crossed make your body match theirs, then uncross your arms usually the customer will do the same thing.

I was having a rough day and I was tired from not sleeping well. The last thing I wanted to do was go to the store but I needed a few things. The store was busy and I wasn't in the mood for people and the more I went through the store the tougher it got for me to find a smile. Going down one aisle was a little old lady who was struggling. I just about turned around and went down a different aisle, but instead, I went over to help her. As I asked her if she could use some help, she looked up at me with a smile. "I wish I could say I didn't need help but I seem to be shrinking in my old age."

I laughed and said, "I hear you. My mom seems like she is 3 inches shorter."

The lady laughed as I handed her the item she was trying to reach. She turned and said to me "Thank you. My husband used to bring me to the store every week to get my groceries. These trips are hard for me because he isn't here anymore, and my health is failing."

I asked her if she had a cell phone and she said "No." I asked her if I could see her grocery list and wrote my number on it. I told her that if she ever needed someone to help her with her grocery shopping to call me and I would gladly come.

Not only did the interaction with her make me feel better but it also gave me an idea. What if on Seniors Day you had a staff member or two whose sole purpose was to help these seniors who are struggling with shopping and give them not only the help, they needed but the company they were missing?

I read a post a while ago on Instagram or Facebook about a young man trying to get his dad to set up online banking and auto-deposit for his pension checks. He also let him know he could have his groceries delivered. I loved the response his dad gave.

"Well, son you see if the check gets deposited directly into my account I wouldn't need to go out and get the mail. Once I got the check in the mail, I would have no reason to go to the bank and see the smiling faces of the tellers. And I would have no reason to go to the grocery store and have Millie the cashier asks how you and my grandkids are doing, and I wouldn't know her husband had recently beat cancer or that they were going on a trip. You see son if I stop going out, I lose those small interactions and connections then what do I have left to live for?"

I feel like this is the same for staff at stores. Humans are meant to be social and interact with each other. The more we shop online the fewer interactions we get. How enjoyable would your day be if you couldn't interact with a single person?

My current job has me working from home and I don't see many people, but I spend most of the day on the phone talking to customers. Without these interactions, I don't believe I could do it.

I remember when I was younger, I worked in a small coffee shop in my little town and every day we had several groups of seniors, farmers, and others who would come in for a cup of coffee early and would never order anything else. There were lots of times they didn't tip either. Many of the younger staff hated to serve them because for them if there was no tip it wasn't worth anything. Don't get me wrong - every dime mattered to me, but the feeling these groups gave me was worth it. Many of them were probably just looking for someone to chat with and the odd day I would even stand by the table and join the conversation. I learned a lot of really neat things about them as people and still to this day love to see them on the street.

Sometimes we have to not look at what we are selling and the final item, but the reason the person is there, and remember you may be the light in a customer's week. We hear a lot about people struggling to cope in life. The way they are treated by you and your business may be the difference between them coping and not coping.

Scenario Nine

Ordering online isn't always more convenient or better for the customer. It seems to be getting harder to get service when you order online as well. How many companies no longer have a phone number you can call, only an email that goes nowhere?

My husband has worn a certain type of cologne for years, and the last few years we could only find it at Christmas time, but last year there was none. I looked online and found it, but they wouldn't ship it to Canada. I bought him another brand to try but he hasn't found anything he likes as much as that cologne. One night he said he found it online, so I placed an order. It was coming from the same place I had tried previously but I tried again with the same result. He kept looking and found it on another website. It's a major supplier so I agreed to try to order it. I placed the order, and it said it would take six weeks to arrive.

As I had mentioned before I can't ship directly to my house, so I chose the pick-up in-store option. Six weeks passed and our order arrived. I went to the store to get it and at the customer service counter let the lady know what I was there for. She angrily informed me that I was supposed to call ahead to pick up orders. I had missed this in all the fine print on the lengthy emails that I received. She picked up the phone and handed it to me to call. I called the number and someone from the back of the store brought my packages up to the front, handed them to me and walked away. I looked at the lady and asked her if I needed to sign something. She said no and walked away. Annoyed, I decided that I no longer needed the other items I had planned to pick up that day and left.

Excited when I got home that I had the cologne my husband wanted. I opened the boxes only to find the wrong brand was shipped, it wasn't what I ordered. Hoping I wouldn't have to ship the items back to get a refund, I looked for a number to call on the order nothing. I did read that I could return the product to the location where I picked it up if it was under $250 Canadian. My daughter was headed into town, so she took them with her and got to the counter. The lady looked at her and said, "You can't return that here." My daughter let her know that we were shipped the wrong product and should get a refund. The lady behind the counter informed her "You can't return that here and good luck getting any sort of refund from our online website."

So, home she came frustrated. A few days later I went to town and had a picture of the policy from the website on my phone. When I got to the counter a different lady than I had seen before asked if she could help. I explained it was an online order, but the website said if it was under $250 Canadian I could return it there and that I was shipped the wrong product. She looked at me and apologized right away and then said, "I have only been working here for a little while so it will take me a few minutes to remember how to do it but let's try."

I appreciated her honesty, and I was more than patient while she made multiple attempts to get into the system. After she got the system to open, it wasn't working properly. She let me know that she was having trouble and was sorry but that she would call her manager over. The manager came and they looked at the items and completed the refund process on the computer. The lady then let me know that it doesn't print anything, but she would gladly take a picture of it with my phone, so I had the information and confirmation of return.

As the manager was leaving, I called her back and let her know I appreciated their help and explained what had happened a few days before with my daughter. She apologized and asked if I knew what time it had been so she could address it.

Same process 2 different people one was willing to give uncommon service and one just didn't care.

Scenario Ten

I remember standing in line in a busy store while a lady was trying to do an exchange and there was a balance owed to her for the exchange. The store only allowed you to complete the refund back to the same card it was bought on, but the customer's card had expired. She had a new one, but the clerk was adamant that she had no way to complete the refund.

The lady was frustrated, which I can understand, and the clerk was unable to think outside of the box how to deal with the issue. In the meantime, the line behind her was growing. The customers in the line were starting to get impatient and the clerk was getting frustrated as was the lady in the line...

After about 15 min the clerk threw her hands up and said I don't know what you want me to do.

The next person in line behind her suggested, "Can you refund the remainder to a gift card for her? Maybe that would work."

"No, it is not the same card I can't" the clerk snapped at her.

Finally, a manager seemed to hear the commotion and saw the large lineup. She inquired what the issue was, and the clerk explained it to her. "I've run into this before. It is tough when it happens but what you do is refund it all to a gift card and then charge the new one on the gift card. The remainder of the credit will stay on the gift card. "

The lady agreed that would be fine and they proceeded to get it taken care of. Now remember this was 30 minutes later and there is a lineup of those that haven't left yet. The manager headed back to wherever she came from, leaving a lineup still for the clerk to deal with.

There are so many things that could have improved this situation.

- The clerk could have called her manager right away when there was an issue.
- The manager of the store should have had a plan for when it is busy, and they could have called another cashier to the tills to help with the lines.

Technology can improve a business, but it can also slow it down immensely. I have seen many situations like the one above where something that should be simple is tied up by technology. Have a good look at your technology partners. Do they make it easier to do business or harder?

A great example of technology working to the store's advantage is my mechanic. This is the same mechanic who fixed my daughter's truck so quickly. He sends me a text when work is done, and the bill is attached. All I have to do is click pay now and it asks for my credit card and pays the bill. It doesn't get much easier than that.

Some examples of things that make it harder are:

- Do you have price checker machines, but they don't work all the time?
- Do you have an online ordering site, but the stock is incorrect or not connected and the customer needs to call for availability anyway?
- Do you have issues with cookies that cause the customer to get errors or a site that isn't mobile-friendly? Fewer

customers have a personal computer nowadays they use their phones or iPads.
- Do your security parameters stop your staff from doing their jobs properly? Is there an option to give the staff the access they need while still protecting confidential information?

Scenario Eleven

I work from home with my current occupation, and I deal with a lot of digital communication through the Teams app, messages, emails, or texts.

Today my phone auto-corrected and told a customer that I could do something that I definitely can't do. It made me look bad and frustrated the customer. We are all guilty of communication issues and misunderstandings when we are talking via digital.

I notice that the more frustrated a customer gets the more we choose to talk to them digitally. I think it's our way of protecting ourselves, but if there is already a communication breakdown adding more emails can create more issues.

Such as today, I had an email come through from a frustrated customer and we quickly responded. However, the response made the situation worse because it made the customer feel like we hadn't dealt with or resolved any of the prior issues. I quickly called the person who had dealt with the current problem to explain how it had come across to me and she said that no, that wasn't what she meant. I let her know to call the customer to clarify before it made the situation worse.

In the time it took to write the initial email and deal with the barrage of issues it caused, a phone call could have been made and a follow-up email with a recap sent.

What the person who wrote the email didn't realize was that this was causing strain in other areas of doing business with the customer who had lost faith in us as a team.

I had a vendor who had been looking for payment for some services that were completed and one of our staff was kind enough to send an email to the correct person and the vendor at the same time to help get them in contact with the correct person. Some emails had gone back a fourth to get the issue resolved and the vendor followed up a few weeks later asking about the payment. The initial person sent an email back asking to be removed from this email chain, as they had nothing to do with it now. It wasn't the person's intention, but it ruffled the feathers of the vendor because it felt like they didn't care. It would have been better to ignore the email and put it in the trash.

I know we all get overwhelmed with emails and sometimes one more seems like too much but think about the other person before you act.

I have a rule for any email when I'm frustrated, or it is a sensitive situation. I don't send that email without waiting 24 hours to decide.

1. Should I send it?
2. Was it just me who reacted this way?
3. Is it better to make a phone call so that true tonality can be heard, and things don't get misconstrued?

A time that the technology can be a huge advantage is when you take something over from someone you can quickly shoot an email or a text so the customer knows you're working on it and the person who passed it on has the confidence that it was taken care of.

Scenario Twelve

Today I was extra proud of the team surrounding me. I got a text and pictures from a customer clearly showing me he had received the wrong piece. His order was correct except for this item. The problem was the customer was 2 hours from the nearest one of our stores and was currently unable to run his business without the piece. I sent out the request for help and quickly the whole team came to the table. We ensured the correct piece was available, then got it organized and the customer sent me a pin where he was located. We called a cab and sent it to his location 2 hrs away at no cost to him. Yes, it probably cost my team around $200 to $300 but this customer was happy and will tell his friends how quickly we fixed his issue. Will he come back to me in the future? Yes, he will.

If I had made him drive the 2 hours each way to get the new piece, he certainly wouldn't have been happy. If we had told him, it wasn't available. Imagine the reaction. No, instead we stepped up and made it happen.

I had another instance where my customer got the wrong part and I hopped in my truck and personally delivered the part to him.

If there is no way to get the item to the customer, give them something in addition to it when available or a discount on their next order. That is always something I like to do when we make a mistake. It requires the customer to give you another chance to show him or her the service your customer is expecting.

Scenario Thirteen

In my company, we have an auto-ship program to help our customers with the services on their equipment. The simple theory behind the program is that we will monitor their equipment and send them prepackaged kits for each service, so it arrives just as maintenance needs to be completed.

The program is great in theory, but it has some critical issues: the customer assumes we will fulfill our promises and send the kits out. If the person monitoring the units doesn't catch that the service is due or if the system doesn't notify the person because the unit isn't reporting hours, we don't send the kit.

The other downside is that because there are so many customers on the program the number of kits to be built is significant. It can take up to two weeks to get the kit built due to a backlog. This causes issues when we need kits quickly which we run into. How can this program be managed to prevent service drops, and keep the customers happy?

It requires a lot of people to manage it and checks and balances in place to prevent issues.

Perhaps there is a better way to take care of the customers such as a different version of the same program without the need for as many people to monitor it? This is where it becomes critical to look at business practices and ensure they are helping the customer, not hindering them.

Scenario Fourteen

I'm in sales and it was the first day of my holidays. I was up before the rest of the family and decided to finish up a couple of things that would be floating until after Christmas.

I had completed everything on the quote except there was one issue with me supplying the product within the rush timeline the customer wanted for the product. I managed to find a similar product and got all the details together then let the customer know that if he was ordering the full package, I would add a discount to the package. He was happy with my answer and took the proposal to his upper management. All without disruption to my family over that first morning of my holidays.

What is so uncommon about this you ask?

- I was on holiday and most people would leave the details for when they came back.
- I know you need to take a holiday, but it took 30 minutes on the first day when I wasn't busy with anything.
- What I didn't tell you was the customer on this account is being moved to another rep on the first of the year and this order wouldn't be completed before that exchange. I believe that respect and courtesy required I complete the task before the exchange. At least if the customer chooses not to order I have done everything in my power. I have realized that the more you help others the more they will try to help you in return.

Scenario Fifteen

Many large companies extend credit to their customers because they are purchasing regularly, and it makes sense to accept payment once a month rather than process it on every transaction.

This is one area I regularly see companies lose customers. I had one customer come to me complaining that we were always telling her she owed us money but that she was constantly writing checks and couldn't get the statements to match.

I connected her with our accounting team, and they kept telling her she still owed money. I could see where it looked like she should be sitting with a credit. At this point I could have wiped my hands of the situation but instead I asked for copies of all the invoices and went to sit down with the customer. After talking to her I realized they were paying their invoices by order number as well as by invoice number and our accounting team was only applying the ones to the invoices, so the customer had a huge credit for double paying.

We would have never figured out the issue if I hadn't taken the time to go through it with the customer.

Every department has an impact on the customer and as businesses we need to look at our processes to ensure every department and person is working towards the same goal, making the customer happy. It's like rowing a boat - if one oar is going one way, and the other is going the opposite the boat will spin or slow down. Too often the boat is not in sync, and it creates customer dissatisfaction.

These same issues also come when you have a business that is very siloed or departmentalized. One department doesn't know what the other is doing, and they are only responsible for their metrics so to make sure their metrics look good they do what is best for them and not the company as a whole.

Section Two

In all of the previous scenarios you will notice some key issues that have created the service problems.

- Communication
- Urgency
- Process and technology
- Empowerment of staff
- Relationship Building and Maintenance
- Employee Engagement and satisfaction
- Listening. Skills

Communication:

Communication is the number one issue in customer service. When communication breaks down customers can't properly be served.

Let's talk about communication. There are many types of communication. But I'm going to break it down into three types:

1. Verbal
   a. Everything we say and hear.
   b. This is everything from the tone of our voices to the way we discuss or don't discuss things.
   c. Saying hello and thank you to your customers.
   d. Asking genuine questions about them and their business are typically the main ideas we think about when we talk about communication. There are also parts of communication we don't think about.

2. Non Verbal
   a. Everything that happens without speaking.
   b. It is body language.
   c. Facial expressions, actions, or lack of action by either you or the customer.

3. Digital
   a. Everything we receive or send and receive from emails, texts, and marketing.

When we communicate with our customers, we. Need to clearly understand what they need from us and what we can do for them. When this doesn't happen is most often when we run into customer service issues.

How do we do this?

- Take your time
- Connect with the customer
- Manage expectations
- Make it easy to do business with you
- Be positive
- Be consistent
- Be approachable

Take your time:

Be timely – don't keep them waiting. Make a viable schedule and stick to it.

Connect with the customer:

Ask them something to break the ice:

For example: How was your drive? Mention the weather.

Actively listen to your customers and ask them the questions.

Rephrase back to the customer what you believe they said to ensure you clearly. understood what they were saying.

Ask questions to understand, not just to respond.

What can we do to service you better?

What can we do to make it easier for you to shop with us?

Where can I be a benefit to your business?

Do something with the responses!

Manage expectations:

Be clear as to what you can do and when you can make it happen.

There are times when you can't meet the customer's exact needs but if you set the expectations up front the customer is more likely to understand.

Don't just tell the customer I can't. Explain to them the circumstances around why it is difficult to make it happen.

For example: I don't have stock on this item, but I can get it from my supplier for you by tomorrow. Can you wait until tomorrow?

(I have clearly set the expectation and asked if that will work for the customer.)

Another way to set the expectations is to let them know what to expect during a visit to your establishment. Let them know that parking is limited, or they may have to pay to park, so they leave a little extra time.

(I have set the expectation that the customer might need cash or a card to pay for parking and that they won't be able to arrive at the time of the appointment and get right in.)

Advise new customers that they should arrive a few minutes early to fill in paperwork, let them know other details like wearing loose-fitting clothing or requiring a driver after. I always like it when a new place asks me if I have ever been there before.

When possible, exceed the customer's expectations.

For example: If you tell them it will be ready in 2 hours but you are half an hour early you have just exceeded their expectations.

Make it easy to deal with you:

Be transparent. When our customers feel we are hiding something from them, they become less understanding and forgiving.

(For example, if you have to send something to another location to repair it make sure you let the customer know.)

Don't blame your mistake on someone else. Own up to it

The best thing you can do is say, "I'm sorry, I made a mistake this is what I'm going to do to fix it."

(We're all human and mistakes happen but it is how you fix the mistake that is your success.)

You do a lot of things the customer isn't even aware of. Sometimes we need to let the customers know what we have done for them to make them see we are helping them.

For example: I was out of stock on that part so I called 3 or suppliers to see if I could get it faster for you.

(By doing this you have shown your customer the effort you put in and saved them the time of calling around as well.)

Get others involved. When you don't know the answer or can't answer the question, get others who have the knowledge involved.

I don't mean to hit the transfer button and send them to another department. I mean. Let the customer know. I don't know the answer but let me find out and ask them if they want to hold or wait depending if they're in person or on the phone, would they like you to call them back.

It's ok to not have all the answers and any reasonable customer wants the correct answer not just a fast answer.

I do this all the time and rarely do I have an issue with a customer being upset but I also learn a lot of things that I don't know currently because I take the initiative to find the answer and relay it to the customer and it makes it easier to do my job in the future.

In the case you need to pass something off to someone else, give the customer a timeline and let them know that if they haven't gotten a response to please call you back or better yet follow up with the customer to ensure the are taken care of. There have been many situations I followed up on that no one got back to the customer, and I was able to catch it before the customer became upset or we lost the sale.

Keep your promises. A promise you make to a customer can be as simple as letting them know you will call or text them when something is ready or telling the customer when it will be done.

Start by making sure the promise you make is something you can control. Don't tell them you will call them in 2 hours if you are off shift in one hour. You're already setting yourself up to fail. Let them know you will call them first thing when you're back the next day or will leave a message for a colleague to call when it is ready. Just in case they don't see the message, suggest they call back at a certain time.

Do what others don't. How often can you do something that another company won't? Deliver the item to your customer or put a thank-you card or small gift in the bag.

Did you know that at Disneyland, staff are empowered to replace any child's ice cream if it falls off the cone?

Something I believe in as a salesperson is letting customers know when I can save them money. I want to be sure they get a discount when there is one, even if they don't know about it. I have called my customers to let them know I had an opportunity to save them money. Simply by saying "No pressure but I wanted you to know because it could save large amounts of money." This has created a trust and relationship with my customers that means they know I will always look out for their best interests.

There is a story on the internet about a young boy who forgot his teddy at a hotel. The story says the father called the hotel and the staff quickly found the teddy. But instead of just returning him, he came with a letter and pictures showing that the teddy had a grand adventure with many hotel staff - one in the restaurant, another by the pool, also with the doorman. You get my picture?

Great customer service doesn't have to cost an arm and a leg. You can reduce marketing dollars by offering great service because word-of-mouth travels.

Look for those outside the box solutions. Sometimes it is good to step back and see what others from different industries are doing. Can you use any of their customer service techniques to improve your business? In my last job I used to be responsible for training in car dealerships. I went in to see where there was opportunity to improve and make recommendations. The best part was I was able to see what stores were doing really well and really poorly across the country. Then I could recommend the changes, based on what I saw working.

I had a customer at one of the stores who had three delivery trucks on the road and they were always out. They always had customers calling in wanting to know how long an order would be. The parts person needed to go to the back of the store, find the order, determine what driver had it and call for an ETA. It was a painful process.

When I ran my store, we had a program that connected to the CRM/invoices which built efficient routes and showed in real time where the drivers were. I showed the dealer what it did and let them know it was reasonably priced. They quickly implemented it, and it has saved them thousands while increasing their customer satisfaction drastically.

Make every customer feel like they are your only customer. There is nothing worse than a customer who feels like a number. Make them feel like they matter. Why do you think take-out companies ask for your name when you order a coffee? It helps them track the orders - but it also makes you feel like you matter and aren't just another number. Would the experience be the same if they called out "Order 42."? I doubt it would be as warm and fuzzy.

I don't tell customers I'm helping someone else. I let them know it will take me a few minutes and I will get them an answer. The more they feel like they are your priority the better the experience they will get.

When customers are happy, look to see what it was that made them happy. Was it you and your service? Did you go above and beyond? Was it communication? Was it something small? Can that be replicated when dealing with other customers?

Be Positive

Look for ways to be positive. I tend to be a glass half full person but my daughter on the other hand wasn't that way by nature. She will get pulled into negative attitudes of others around her and there tends to be a lot of negativity going around her office recently. She could tell it was affecting the way she worked and her overall health. We had a great conversation about finding a way to avoid being pulled into the negative conversations and I even asked her to look at herself and see if she was fueling the negativity. She told herself she was going to start avoiding the negative people in the office the best she could and remove herself from the situations as they happened. She started to listen to upbeat happy music through her headphones and told herself she was in charge of being happy. It helped make it better to go to work and quickly others in the office started to do the same. Which in turn helped her office's morale and customer satisfaction.

You can lead change.

How often do we complain about where we work and the things that aren't working in our stores? How can you influence without authority? Become an expert and pass it on. Position yourself as the go-to person. Lead by example.

Build meaningful relationships with people ranging from managers to co-workers. Truly get to know the people you work with. Build common bonds. These people can become your success or can stand in the way depending on your relationship.

People resist change and need to know why something is changing or why it's being done a different way. Let other be part of the solution and change. Ask for their suggestions.

Conclusion

There is nothing magical in what I have outlined in this book. It has just become uncommon for people to do the things in the book and go the extra step or mile for a customer.

If you want to be one of the top 10% of people and or businesses, I recommend you take stock of your daily activities and the interactions with customers within your store or business. It is easy when you are on the inside to look and say everything is great. Take the time to see things from a consumer's perspective.

Just like in the scenario about the service shipping program, the program was created to service the customers better but wasn't doing as it was intended it was making it worse. There are lots of things that seem like they are great for customers in theory but when you step into the customer's shoes they may not be so great.

One of the best managers I know was in charge of Change Management in our organization and he always told me "Our business has a shelf life. The customer expects the service they get each time they come in. If nothing changes the value of the service goes down because it isn't new or fresh and doesn't feel like you're doing more for them."

It's the same reason fast food drive thru's started to run two lanes. The customers expected to get through as quickly as possible and it gives the feeling that they are getting through faster. I can't say if it is or is not but it feels that way.

One thing you may have noticed is that customer service all boils down to how you make the customer feel. Do they feel like you care about them and their business? When we give poor service, it feels like we don't care.

Do the work! Often the difference between good and great is extra effort. Be willing to go one step past what others would be willing to do.

There is nothing worse than hearing it's not my job. Creating a business that customers want to do business with is your job no matter what part of the company you're in. Sometimes it's as simple as taking the customer to the person that can help them, not just pointing fingers and sending them somewhere else.

One of my favourite things is to learn. Most times when I can't answer a question or help a customer find the information myself I follow through and it becomes part of my knowledge base. It shows the customer that they matter to me. I have never had one customer get mad at me when I said, "I don't know the answer but let me find out and get back to you." They will respect your honesty, and most people don't care that you don't have all the answers, but they do care that you help them get them.

When you do tell them you will find out and get back to them, do so. I don't know how many times I have said to a customer, "I just wanted to touch base and let you know that I haven't got the answer yet, but I'm still working on it." What does this tell your customer? You care and you haven't just swept it under the rug. Silence is deadly when it comes to customer service. It means you didn't care enough to finish getting the information they needed or fix the problem.

Does your company have those customers or staff members that no one wants to deal with?

I love helping these customers! Looking back at Scenario 6, I took it upon myself to make it a challenge to make this customer happy. Challenge yourself to do the same.

Copy the best
You go into your local small business and the person behind the counter has the ability to make you feel welcome or make you want to never go back. Help your customer make their buying decision by remembering the best customer service experience you have ever had. Then try to copy that.

Focus on the customers needs not your own

Have you ever had a customer come in and ask for something very specific? Did you take the time to ask them more questions? Why are they looking for this specific item? What need is it filling? Does it need to be exact or would something similar do? When do they need it for?

When things go wrong
Look at the situation from the outside. Most times we are to close to the issue to make a good decision. In our training course we use the Q-Tip method. Quit Taking It Personally!

Watch for Trigger words
Certain words such as you, don't, policy, or that's not my job cause conflict. Replace these words with I, we, absolutely. You will instantly reduce the conflict and build confidence.

Create your streaks

Treat your customer like your snap chat streaks. Make them a priority, don't lose them, find any way you can to keep that streak.

www.ingramcontent.com/pod-product-compliance
Lightning Source LLC
Chambersburg PA
CBHW070358230526
45471CB00006B/2622